The Pilgrim Fathers

Frederick W. Nolan

by

kland

Macdonald
Educational

Who were the Pilgrim Fathers?

The Pilgrim Fathers came from a little village called Scrooby in Nottinghamshire, England. They were Puritans. Puritans were groups of strict people who wanted to change the ways of the Church of England.

King James I was the head of the Church of England. He ordered everyone to obey the rules of the Church of England and go to their services. Anyone who refused to obey the laws was punished.

Look carefully at these two pictures. This one shows a Church of England service at the time of James I. The priest wears robes.

The people are all carrying a prayer-book, from which all prayers were read. Notice all the decoration in the church.

The Puritans thought that church services should be very simple. They did not think that the ministers should wear robes nor that there should be any special ceremonies.

The Puritans did not like the Church of England so they refused to attend any of their services. They were fined and threatened with jail.

The Scrooby group organised their own services. They were held at the home of their leader, William Brewster. They met every Sunday to read from the Bible and to discuss what they had read.

This picture shows the Scrooby group's meeting. The people are wearing plain and simple clothes. The only book used is the Bible.

The leader, called an Elder, reads a passage from the Bible. Their meeting is much simpler than the Church of England service.

The Puritans escape

People in Holland were allowed to live and worship as they liked. Some of the Scrooby group decided to go and set up new homes there, but at that time, it was against the law to leave England without the king's permission.

The group had to make secret arrangements with the captain of a small ship to take them to Holland. But the captain betrayed them to the king's officers. The group was arrested as they went on board. Their belongings were taken away. The men were put in prison for a month. A year later, in 1608, they tried to escape again.

A Dutch shipowner agreed to pick them up from the lonely marshes on the coast. The women and children went from Scrooby down the river by boat, but the men walked there. The women arrived first, so their boat waited in a sheltered place. When the tide went out, the boat stuck on a mud bank.

Next day, the Dutch ship arrived and some of the men went aboard. Suddenly the captain saw soldiers approaching. He quickly set sail leaving the women stranded in their boat. The women were arrested. Later they were set free and went to Holland too.

Life in Holland

In Holland, the Puritans settled in Amsterdam. They did not like living there very much. They were country people and found it hard to find work they could do in a city. They had to learn a new language, and new jobs and skills. They had expected to make friends with other Puritans there, but found instead that they did not agree with them about the way they should worship.

Leyden

They moved to a smaller town called Leyden. They worked hard and earned enough money to buy a house and some land. The house was used as a church and a meeting place, as well as a home for their new leader John Robinson, and his family.

The group stayed in Leyden for ten years. But they were still not content. They were afraid their children would forget they were English and that they would not live the simple life that the Puritans believed in.

Some of the group became wheelwrights.

Others became hatters, glovers, weavers or tailors.

William Brewster became an English teacher. He also learned how to be a printer.

He set up a printing press and printed Puritan pamphlets which he smuggled to England.

Plans to leave

The Puritans wanted to remain English, but they also wanted to be able to worship in their own way and govern themselves. Their only answer was to find a place where they could live as they wished and yet still remain English.

They decided to go to America because part of the land there belonged to England, and very few people lived there. America in those days was not like it is today. It had no big towns, no ports, no farms, or cattle. The only people who had always lived there were the Indians.

Jamestown, the first English settlement in North America.
It was founded in 1607 by the Virginia Company of London.
The reports the Pilgrim Fathers read about Jamestown
persuaded them that America would be a good place to live.

A few Spanish, French and
English people had started
settlements in America. The
English had claimed a large
area of land on the east coast,
which they called Virginia. It
was ruled by a special company,
which was chosen by the English
king, James I.

The Puritans decided to go
to Virginia to start their own
settlement.

It was very expensive to
go on a voyage like this and
start a settlement. Ships were
needed and so were tools and
stores. The group had very little
money, so they asked some
merchants to help them.

The merchants loaned them
money, and found them an area
of land where they could settle.

The group promised to work
five days a week for seven
years to pay back the money
they had borrowed.

The king, James I, gave them
permission to leave England
and settle in America.

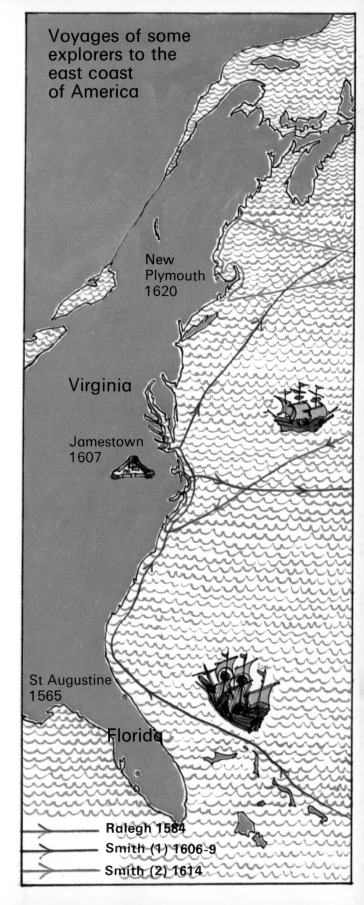

Voyages of some
explorers to the
east coast
of America

New
Plymouth
1620

Virginia

Jamestown
1607

St Augustine
1565

Florida

→ Ralegh 1584
→ Smith (1) 1606-9
→ Smith (2) 1614

The Mayflower sets sail

The group bought a ship called the Speedwell and hired another ship called the Mayflower. They left Leyden and sailed back to England in the Speedwell. The other ship, the Mayflower, was waiting for them at Southampton in England, with another group of people who also wanted to start a new life in America. These passengers were nicknamed 'Strangers' because they were mostly members of the Church of England. The Puritans were nicknamed 'Saints'. There were 120 passengers in all.

The two ships set sail on August 5th 1620. The Speedwell started leaking and the ships had to go into harbour at Plymouth so she could be repaired. In the end it was decided to abandon the Speedwell. Some people, upset by all the troubles and delays, decided not to go on the voyage.

All the spare provisions and the 100 remaining passengers crammed aboard the Mayflower and at last, on September 6th, 1620 they set sail.

The Puritans looked on their voyage as a pilgrimage to a new world. This is why they are known as the Pilgrim Fathers.

Aboard the Mayflower

The Mayflower was a very small ship. She was only about 25 metres long and 7 metres wide. The captain and some of his crew had cabins; but everyone else was crowded on the open deck with all their baggage. They probably slept on straw mattresses. The hold below was packed with tools, weapons, barrels of gunpowder and all sorts of provisions, such as dried peas, salt meat, flour, grain and hard biscuits. They also took fishing equipment, blankets, ropes and extra clothing. They had to take everything they needed since they did not know what they would find when they arrived in America.

The voyage took two months. At first the weather was fine, but halfway across the Atlantic there were heavy storms. All the passengers crowded below the decks, in case the huge waves swept them overboard. The sails tore and one of the main beams cracked and came out of place. The men managed to force it back into place and supported it with a strong post.

The journey was horrible. Everyone was seasick and for most of the time they were wet and cold, cramped and hungry. They prayed to God and sang hymns to keep up their spirits.

Surprisingly, only one man died. Even more surprisingly a baby was born on the voyage. He was named Oceanus.

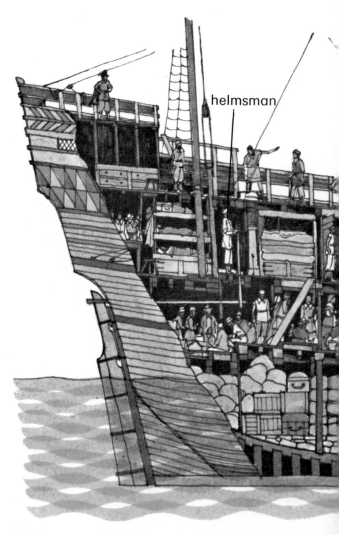

helmsman

the Mayflower   the Spirit of London

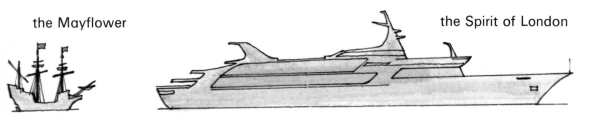

Compare the size of the Mayflower with a modern ocean going liner.

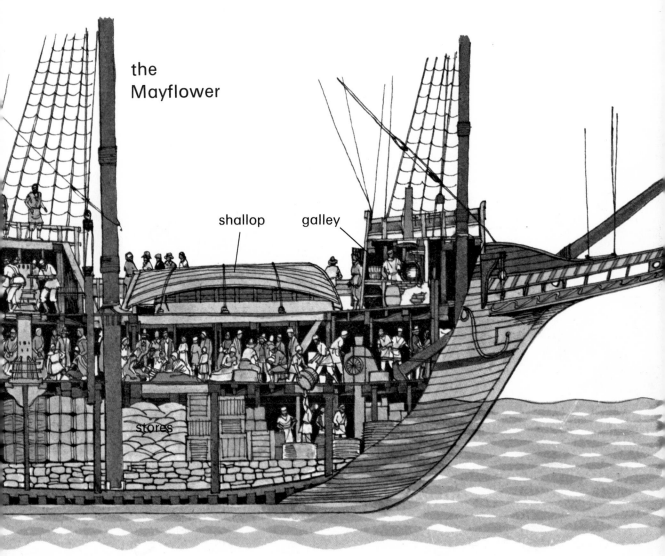

the
Mayflower

shallop   galley

stores

The Mayflower Compact

On November 9th, the Pilgrims saw land. When they looked at their map, they found they had come too far north. They had meant to land in Virginia. They had come to a place called Cape Cod.

The Pilgrims wanted to sail south to the land they had been promised, but the waters were dangerous. They were afraid to go on, so they turned back and anchored in Cape Cod bay.

Nobody was allowed ashore. The leaders decided that first, an agreement should be made about the way the settlement would be run. It was signed by the heads of all the families aboard. This agreement was called the Mayflower Compact.

A landing party went ashore to collect wood for fires and fresh
water to drink. They dug the soil and found it was black and rich.

But Cape Cod was not a suitable place to settle, as the harbour
was far too shallow. It was now November, and the weather was
freezing cold. There was no-one to help or welcome them in this new
land, and they had no warm homes to go to. The living conditions
on the Mayflower were very cramped.

Everyone was longing to get ashore and start building a settlement
before it became any colder. They decide to send out exploring
parties to find a suitable place to settle.

Explorations

1. Sixteen men went ashore. They saw some Indians in the distance.
As soon as the Indians saw them, they ran into the woods.

3. They did not find a good place to settle. Another party set out
in the shallop. They saw more Indians, this time by the water's edge.

5. They sailed into another bay. A storm began.
The mast and rudder broke. The men managed to reach
an island where they could rest for the night.

2. The men followed. They came to an abandoned Indian village. They found remains of houses and graves, and hidden baskets of corn.

4. At night they made camp. Next morning Indians attacked them. The Pilgrims fired muskets and the Indians fled.

6. The next morning they explored the bay. It was deep enough for big ships. The land nearby had already been cleared, the soil seemed rich and there were fresh streams.

Landing at New Plymouth

The exploration party sailed back to the Mayflower with the good news that they had found a suitable site. The next day, the Mayflower sailed there. When it arrived, the Pilgrims agreed it did seem a good place, and decided to call it New Plymouth. The deep bay was full of fish, there were several brooks of clear water, plenty of trees both for building and for fruit, a hill where they could build a fort and lookout posts. Somebody had already cleared the land for farming

It was now midwinter. The Pilgrims were impatient to leave the Mayflower and start building their settlement. Some of the men went ashore to fell trees, and cut stakes of wood to lay out the sites for all the houses. Some of the men kept watch for Indians.

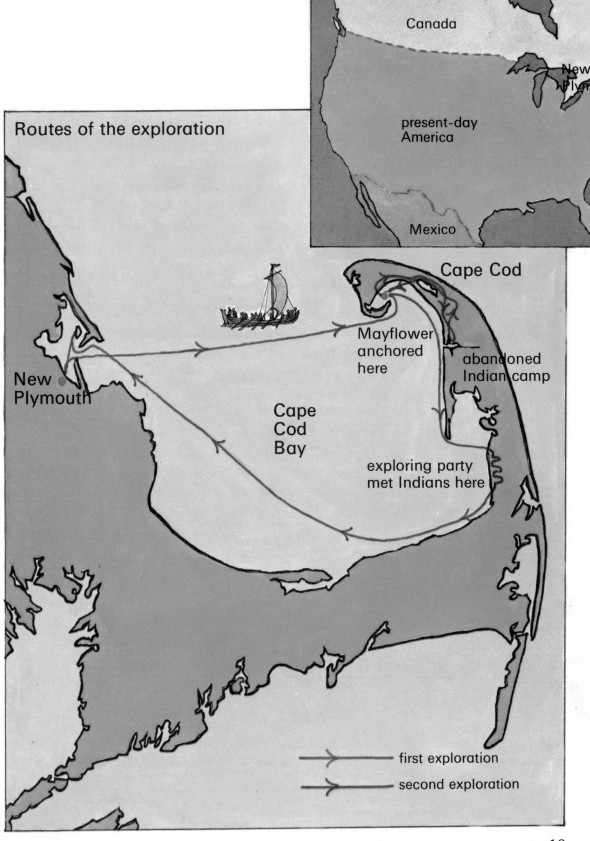

Routes of the exploration

Canada

New
Plymouth

present-day
America

Mexico

Cape Cod

Mayflower
anchored
here

abandoned
Indian camp

New
Plymouth

Cape
Cod
Bay

exploring party
met Indians here

first exploration

second exploration

19

The first homes

On Christmas Day, the Pilgrims began building their first house. This was a small storehouse for their guns, tools and clothes. It took them a long time as the weather was bad and they had few tools.

Many of the Pilgrims lived together in this house. Others made rough huts of branches and sod, or dugouts—which were simply made by digging a hole in the ground or in a hillside, and roofing it with poles and bark.

These shelters had dirt floors and were damp and cold. Nevertheless, the Pilgrims were glad to be ashore and in their own private homes after months aboard the crowded Mayflower.

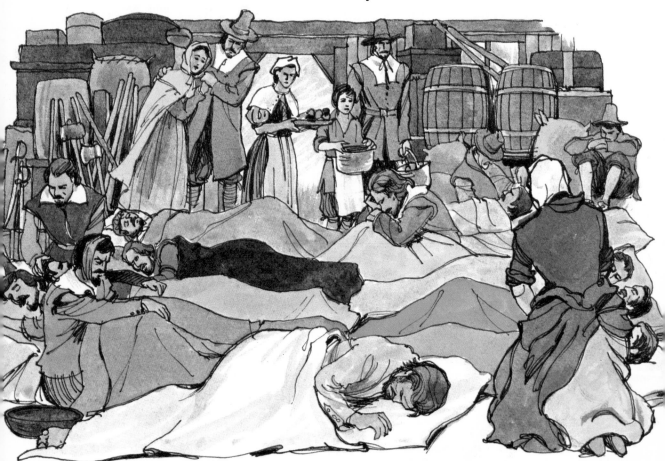

The winter was hard for the Pilgrim settlers. Their work was very hard, and their living conditions were difficult and dirty. Many of the settlers were already weakened by their long stay aboard ship. Most of them got scurvy— which is a disease caused by not having enough fresh fruit and vegetables and some of them fell ill with pneumonia.

Almost every day, somebody died. There were only six or seven people who kept well enough to look after the others. They fetched wood, made fires, cooked, and washed the clothes and bodies of the sick people.

Although they had not seen any Indians since they arrived, nevertheless the settlers were worried that they might be attacked at any time. The dead people were buried without gravestones, so that the Indians would not know how many of the settlers had died. By spring half the settlers had died. The others were still weak, but as the weather became warmer, they recovered.

sod hut

bark and pole hut

inside
bark and pole hut

21

Building new homes

trimming logs with an adze

saw pit

axe

In spring the settlers built timber houses. First they felled the trees and trimmed them into logs with an adze.

The logs were then sawn into planks. When enough planks had been sawn, the men could start building a house.

cellar hole

First they dug a cellar hole and lined it with stone. This would keep the house warm in winter.

The cellar could be used as a frost-proof store for fruit and vegetables.

The frame of the house was put flat on the ground and the parts joined with wooden pins called treenails.

When the frame was ready, the men all got together and lifted it into position.

treenail

Once the frame was up planks were fastened on to it. Any cracks were filled in with clay.

The roof was thatched with rushes.

23

Inside the homes

inside
a Pilgrim's
frame house

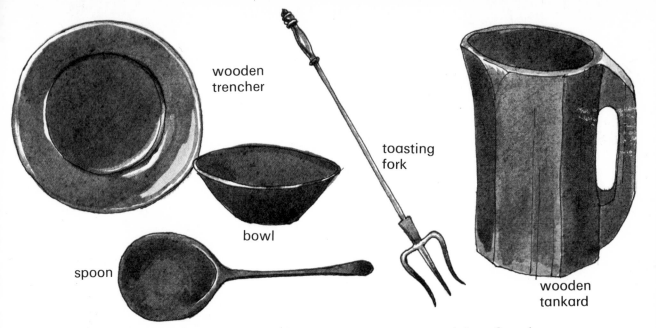

wooden trencher

toasting fork

bowl

spoon

wooden tankard

The houses were very simple. There was one room with a fireplace. This is where the family cooked, ate and slept. The children slept in a small roof loft.

The furnishings were all home-made. There had been no room on the Mayflower for anyone to bring their furniture. There were no rugs or chairs; these were difficult things to make. Most people made rough stools and benches and simple frames for their beds. The beds had ropes for springs and big bags stuffed with rags or feathers were used as mattresses. The settlers also made simple wooden dishes, spoons and mugs, but they had brought iron pots and forks for cooking.

iron trivet

hunting knife

iron pot

rush light holder

skillet

Dutch oven

Work in the settlement

Life in the settlement was hard work. Everybody, even the children, had tasks to do.

Some of the men felled trees for building.

The trees they used were mostly oak or pine.

shaving horse

The men smoothed the logs and cut them into planks.

reeds

The children collected reeds for thatching the roofs.

Throughout the spring, the settlers planted seeds and built houses.

hoe

Some of the settlers made their own farm tools.

They hoed the ground to prepare it for planting.

The settlers sowed barley and peas that they had brought with them from England.

Every family had its own garden where herbs and vegetables could be grown.

Making friends with the Indians

The settlers had not seen any Indians near the settlement. So they were most surprised when, one day in spring, an Indian walked into the village and greeted the amazed settlers in English. He told them that his name was Samoset, and that he had learned English from fishermen who had visited the coast.

The settlers welcomed him and gave him food and drink. Samoset told them that a tribe of Indians had once lived in the place where they had settled. All of this tribe had died of an illness three years earlier. Samoset belonged to another tribe called the Massasoit.

Samoset was sent back to his tribe with presents. He came back with other Indians. The settlers gave them food and the Indians danced to show their friendship.

Several days later Samoset came back with another Indian called Squanto, who also spoke English. Squanto was the only Indian left of the tribe which had died of illness. He had been carried off as a slave to Spain and had escaped to England. This was how he knew English. They told the settlers that Chief Massasoit wanted to visit them. The settlers wanted to be friendly, but they were afraid to let the chief and all his warriors come into the settlement.

Eventually, the governor of the settlement, John Carver, decided to allow Massasoit and twenty of his braves to visit them.

They were taken to a cottage and the governor came to meet them with drummers and trumpeters. The two leaders made peace terms. They agreed not to attack one another and also agreed to help one another if either of them was attacked.

When Massasoit and his braves left, Squanto decided to stay with the settlers. He stayed with them until he died.

Squanto helps

Squanto showed the settlers how to plant Indian corn. He dug holes with a sharp stick and dropped four grains of corn into each one, separated so that they did not touch each other.

He also showed them how to make the soil richer by burying three herrings in each hill of corn. He planted pumpkins between the hills. Their big leaves shaded the soil and kept it damp.

Squanto knew which herbs and plants were good to eat.
He knew how to tap the maple trees for sap. He showed the settlers
how to boil the sap to make it into a sweet syrup.

The settlers wanted to explore the inland rivers
and streams. Their own boats were too big. Squanto
helped them make canoes from birchbark.

31

Summer harvest

hunting

fishing

collecting
berries

raking
oysters

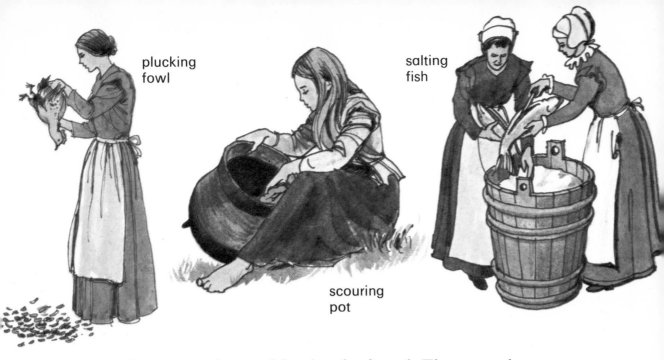

plucking
fowl

scouring
pot

salting
fish

In summer there was plenty of food to be found. The men who were good shots went hunting for wild fowl and deer. Others went fishing for cod or bass, or collected shellfish and wild fruits. The women busily salted fish and dried meat to keep for the winter.

The pea and barley crops did not do very well. The peas shrivelled in the sun and only some of the barley came up. However, the Indian corn, which Squanto had helped the settlers to plant, ripened well.

pounding
corn

cooking
corn cakes

Autumn thanksgiving

With the summer weather everyone recovered from their sickness. By autumn, eleven houses were finished and the corn had been gathered in. The stores of fish, meat, vegetables and corn were all stored away for the winter.

A new governor, William Bradford, arranged a thanksgiving feast to celebrate the harvest and to thank God for their settlement. He sent four men out hunting. They came back with enough wild geese, ducks and turkeys to last a week.

The settlers invited chief Massasoit and 90 of his Indians to the feast. They brought five deer with them.

The feast lasted three days. Great fires were made in the open to cook the deer and the wild fowl.

The women made huge pots of succotash, which was a stew of beans. They also made corn bread. They pounded the corn into meal, mixed water with it and fried the mixture on a griddle. There were also wild fruits to eat and beer to drink made from the barley crop.

New Plymouth

This is how the New Plymouth settlement looked a few years after the Pilgrims had settled.

A strong fort had been built on the top of the hill. Cannons were mounted on the roof and a guard kept watch there night and day. The fort was the biggest building in the settlement. The ground floor was also used as a church, until one was built in 1628.

Since the settlers were worried that other Indian tribes might attack them, they decided to surround the settlement with a strong wooden palisade. This was almost four metres high. Three wooden gates were built at the end of the streets.

A stockade was built in the centre of the settlement. It had guns facing in every direction in case of attack.

When the merchants loaned the Pilgrims money for their voyage, they had made them promise that everything would be shared, and that everybody would work together.

The leaders found that people did not work very hard on land that did not belong to them. They decided to give every family a plot of land outside the village. Each family could grow its own store of corn.

People worked much harder on their own land and produced not only enough corn for themselves but some extra. They traded the corn with the Indians for furs. They sent the furs to England to pay for tools, clothes, and other things which they still needed.

Other Puritans came out from England to join the settlement. By 1627 there were over 200 people living there. By that time, too, the settlers had managed to pay back their loan to the merchants in England.

Although their life was still not easy, the settlers now felt they had overcome the worst problems. Best of all they were free to worship as they wished.

Animals and plants

wild turkey

wild pigeon

wild plum

holly

maple

pine

grapes

deer

cod

oyster

crayfish

eel

bass

watercress

lady's slipper
orchid

Indian
corn

cow
parsley

squash

pumpkin

Follow the Pilgrim Fathers

Play this game with one or two of your friends. You will need a counter each and two dice. Take it in turns to throw the dice. The person who throws the highest number starts. Each person throws the dice in turn. Add together the numbers they show and move your counter that number of spaces.

If you land on a red square follow the instruction beside it. Some squares will help you get on faster. Others will tell you to go back a few spaces. The first person who reaches Thanksgiving is the winner.

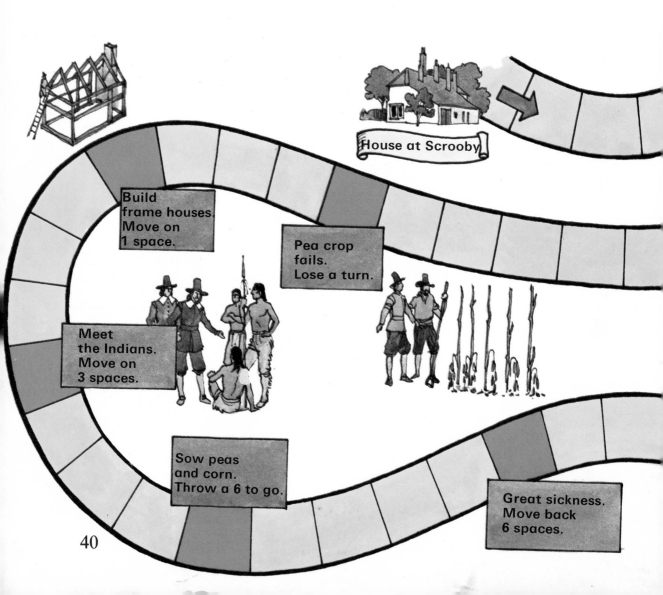

House at Scrooby

Build frame houses. Move on 1 space.

Pea crop fails. Lose a turn.

Meet the Indians. Move on 3 spaces.

Sow peas and corn. Throw a 6 to go.

Great sickness. Move back 6 spaces.

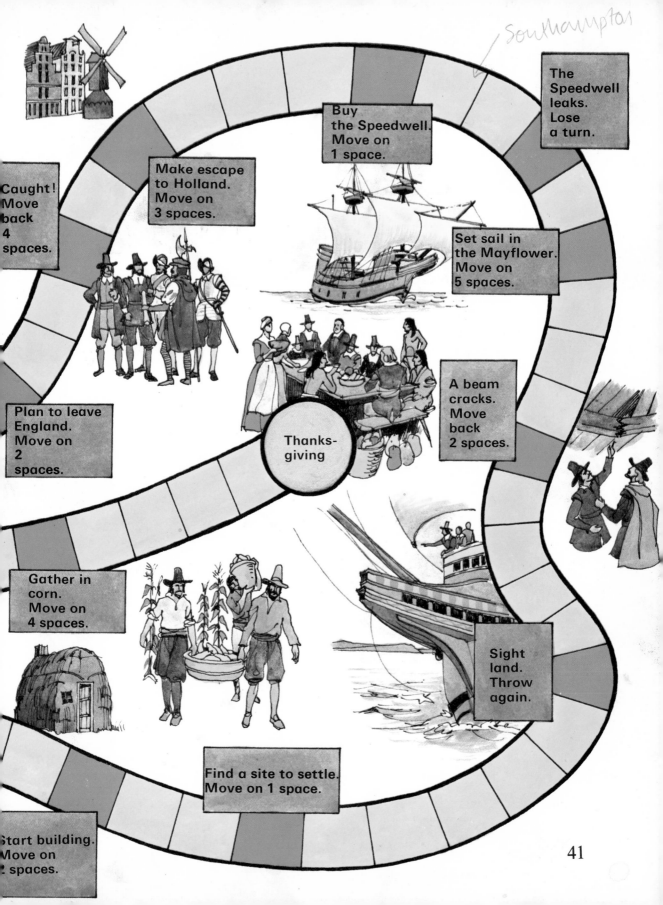

Southampton

The Speedwell leaks. Lose a turn.

Buy the Speedwell. Move on 1 space.

Make escape to Holland. Move on 3 spaces.

Caught! Move back 4 spaces.

Set sail in the Mayflower. Move on 5 spaces.

Plan to leave England. Move on 2 spaces.

A beam cracks. Move back 2 spaces.

Thanks-giving

Gather in corn. Move on 4 spaces.

Sight land. Throw again.

Find a site to settle. Move on 1 space.

Start building. Move on 2 spaces.

41

Map

North America

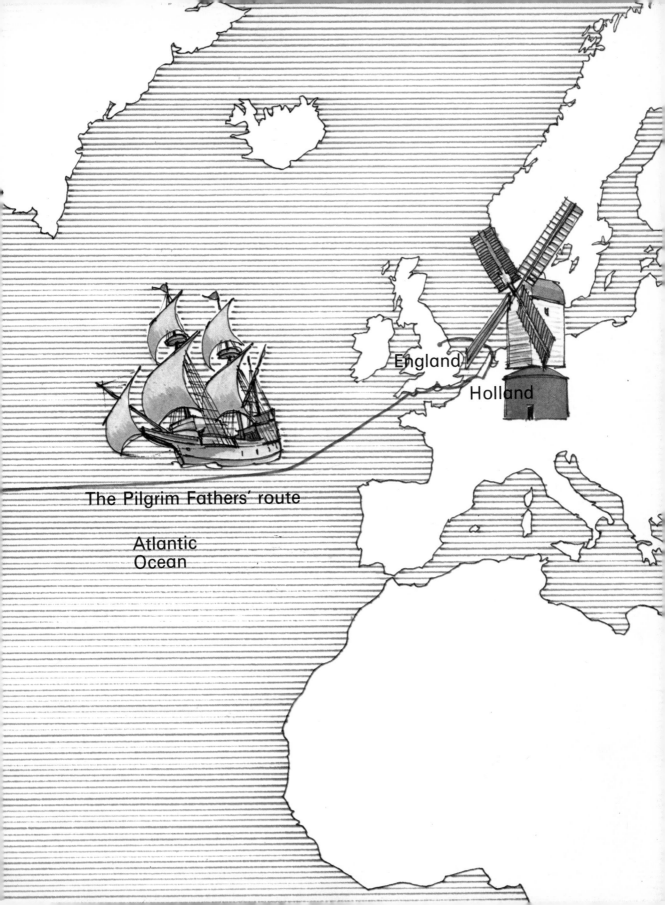

England

Holland

The Pilgrim Fathers' route

Atlantic
Ocean

Index